Forex

The Ultimate Beginner's Guide To Forex and Trading Profitably

by

Henry L. Bernard

All contents of this book are protected by law and unlawful use will be reported to authorities.

Table of Contents:

Part 1: Before You Begin

Introduction – page 5

The History of Forex and Currencies – page 6

The Pentagram of Profits – page 7

The History and The True Value of a Dollar – page 8

How To Invest Income – page 10

History of Investing – page 14

Hedge Funds & Wealth Management – page 18

The Modern Investor – page 20

Part 2: Becoming a Forex Pro

The Fast Road to Becoming a Forex Pro – page 27

The Keys to the Kingdom of Professional Trading – page 28

Nerves of Steel – page 32

Strategy #1: Creating a personal Trading

Periodical – page 35

How To Successfully Analyze a Trading Session – page 40

Part 3: The Profitable Power of Risk Management

Risk Management – page 44

Part 4: The Basics of Reading a Forex Chart

Reading a Forex Chart – page 52

The Most Important Currency Pairs – page 53

QUICKLY NAVIGATING A FOREX CHART – page 55

Forex Climates – page 60

Tracking Market Movement – page 63

Part 5: The Power Of Framing

What in the world is framing? - page 68

Finding the Best Timeframes To Trade On – page 73

Part 6:
The Basics Of Price Action

Price Action And Why It's So Profitable – page 82

Part 7:
How To Enter Profitable Trades

When And Where to Enter the Market – page 88

Symmetrical Triangle Breakouts

Flag Breakouts – page 91

Pennant Breakout – page 93

Knowing When To Pull The Trigger – page 94

How to Minimize Risk – page 96

Part 9:

You're Ready for Your First Trade

<u>Are You Excited?</u> - page 102

Welcome to The Ultimate Beginner's Guide To Forex. Investing is a path that can lead hard working people to financial stability and wealth. But before the first stock is ever traded, it's important to understand the road to financial freedom through personal investing comes through self-discipline and a fundamental understanding of currency, global economy structure, and business.

The Ultimate Beginner's Guide To Forex is a guide specifically designed for someone interested in starting investing or a struggling investor by creating a simple, practical step-by-step blueprint to create a profitable investing strategy. This investing playbook has been fine tuned through years of studies and will eliminate years of frustration, silly trial and error, loss of life savings and even procrastination.

The first of part of the profit playbook sets the foundations for proper investing and money management. Even though this module, The Wonderful History of Currency & Investing looks theoretical at the surface, it's a crucial and practical introduction to trading. It introduces the importance of understanding currency, how we use money on a day to day basis and how to take advantage of the most advanced resources and technology in mankind's history to create profits and how to build a first wealth portfolio.

The Wonderful History of Currency & Investing Module is broken into five main sections that break down the birth of currency all the way to the modern investor.

The five sections are:

1. The History and the Value of a Dollar

2. Exchanging Skill and Labor for Money and Using Extra Income to Make Yourself More Money

3. The History of Investing and Why it's Important to You

4. The Evolution of Hedge Funds and Money Management.

5. The Transformation of the Individual Investor and It's Importance to Exponentially Boost ROI for Investing

Let's get started so we can launch a Profit Playbook as soon as possible.

The History and The True Value of a Dollar

Around 1760 BC, the first documented currency monetary exchange and wage system was created by the 6th king of Babylon. This marked the first official standard for currency in a society and is the original monetary system that founded currency as we see it today.

Today, every job has a specific value assigned by a series of demand in a product directly accompanied with the price it costs to develop the product.

And the value of a job is directly proportionate to the cost of living, the price of necessities weighted against average income and luxuries available in each city and country.

Today, everyone that can read this course uses a currency has an almost unlimited amount of products, goods and services available which means one thing. If you are reading this course you have already created the assets available to become a highly successful investor. You've found a skill and/or labor and have exchanged it for a paycheck. If you've used your paycheck to buy anything ever. You're already an investor and now it's time to use your paycheck to get even better at investing.

Exchanging Skill and Labor for Money and How To Invest Income

When you work for a company, you are directly exchanging both your time and skills to build a specific asset for your employer. In return, the employer exchanges the asset you've created for a paycheck that allows you to pay for a home, car, groceries, utilities and other assets like Internet, TV and entertainment.

As a beginning investor it may not be clear exactly how to use your paycheck to invest especially if you have no money to invest now. The good news is there's a way to free up money and the breakdown is surprisingly simple.

1. Always keep track of the budget. Every penny that you spend and invest adds up over to astronomical numbers throughout a decade. Reviewing a budget weekly, and simply exploring ways to free up money by finding the best value for services available takes about half an hour a week. We tend to be careless with our paycheck but forget the 40 hour workweek we invested to make every $ of that paycheck. Simply tracking where we spend our money and

finding ways to to better ways to invest in bills will automatically create a more profitable investor. Simply creating an objective bird's eye view of asset management will create a more complete understanding of business and investing.

2. Find a home that suits your needs not one that suits your luxurious desires. Finding a proper home can easily create an extra six figures in your wealth portfolio if it's properly invested. All it takes is finding a home that does the job at the most basic levels. Renovations can come with time and within a couple decades actually compounds the original money you freed up from simplifying your home.

3. Understand that food is an overlooked and virtually unheard of asset inside

investing but diet is directly related to energy levels and crucial for the ability to focus. Using fresh fruits and vegetables and eating foods without preservatives will open up production and you'll feel better and shockingly create more happiness. Don't break the bank eating healthy but find ways to invest in healthy food on a cheap budget. Remember, simply staying away from processed foods and preservatives as much as possible will create dramatic shifts in energy and focus.

4. After reflecting and refining your budget, extra money will automatically show up. Split that money half into direct savings and half into investing. As you become a more profitable investor, you can personalize where you invest assets but for now, getting ahead on bills will

protect your investment portfolio during tough financial months. This ultimately allows the highest ROI possible inside of live investments.

Always remember that every dollar matters and never cut corners. The ultimate goal in investing is to enjoy life to it's fullest while being intelligent about acquiring assets.

The History of Investing and Why it's Important to You

We live in a highly advanced civilization with technology and statistics that even the most success traders couldn't fathom two decades ago. So why in the world is important to understand the birth of investing that started in Venice during the 1300s. How could men obtaining and trading business debts and government securities on slates have anything to do with a simple click to acquire stocks?

The answer is simple. The exact purpose of investing has not has not changed since its beginning in the 1300s. As an investor in the 1300s, wealthy individuals bought debts that were documented on slates and then exchanged with other investors to build wealth. Today, investing uses the same exact approach. When an individual buys a stock, he or she ultimately loans a company cash that the company can use for reinvestments and paying debt.

The goal of investing hasn't changed over its 700 years of documented existence. The purpose of investing is simplistic. Investing uses intelligence to find and loan profitable business men, businesses, and markets money in exchange for a small ownership or stake in a company.

Although this idea is simplistic in nature, understanding the culture of value exchange and business investing will boost your investing returns drastically. The random tip offs for quick, exciting trading with high risks seems less appetizing while sticking to smart, disciplined and profitable investing becomes a lot more satisfying.

Remember that every time someone buys an investment inside a company, he or she takes some hard earned cash and directly loans that money to the company to use freely.

It's important to ensure every investment is in safe hands through sound ownership and proven dominance inside of a proven market. Remember companies are open about their businesses once they have secured an innovation inside of a market place and it's important to keep your eyes peeled for sound businesses.

Sound investing always starts with a firm foundation of understanding the fundamentals of business. These foundations aren't complicated but every unsuccessful investor forgets to build foundations on the way to building a wealth portfolio. Sadly when foundations are skipped, years of hard work gets destroyed through the simplest mistake that even the brightest investor can't fix.

We're going to avoid that financial destruction in Beginner's Profit Blueprint. Beginner's Profit Blueprint is about learning sound investing and using timeless fundamentals to create a monstrous and secure investing portfolio no matter whether you're starting with $100 or $100,000.

Remember it's never too late to start investing but there is absolutely NO substitute for consistent, secure and sound investing.

The Evolution of Hedge Funds & Wealth Management

The first known Hedge Fund was started by a gentleman named Alfred Jones in 1948. The Harvard graduate had a simple idea that he used to create professional investing. By investing in long term stocks and using short selling for portfolio security, Jones created a gem for America. He opened up the opportunity for hardworking Americans to invest their money in long term returns while they went about their everyday lives. Americans work hard for their cash and by simply budgeting and freeing up money, families we secured to compound their savings over decades of smart decision making from professional traders.

To this day, using Hedge Funds to build a secure portfolio that thrives through recessions and depressions is a way smarter than stashing away money in a savings account.

But there is no substitution for individual investing. Hedge funds are brilliant at investing but their goal is simple. Consistently build income year after year using ultra safe and sound investments they invest billions of dollars into. This leaves little room for error for the institution, but it doe leave tons of money on the table for individual investors to capitalize off of over the long term.

This brings us to the greatness of individual investing. While the danger is there, there's no substitute for consistent three digit returns within 3 to 6 months . If you play your cards properly and build a Profit Playbook, every year, you'll gain an edge over traditional investing. But it takes discipline, intelligence and a carefully eye on trading experts.

The Transformation of the Modern Investor

Before the internet, individual investing was nearly impossible and even a few years ago, individual trading required some kind of edge. Investors had to read thousands of pages of business plan releases, quarterly earnings reports, employment rates, official economic forecast releases and stacks of other complicated reports to create a single high probability investment.

Thankfully modern investing is easier. Today, investors have to use a new investment skill for an edge. Thousands of pros are paid handsomely to find the most reputable information and to deliver a clean, crisp report for millions of readers to utilize within a minute.

This means that unlike the days of old, the modern investor only has to master one solution to succeed. All that is important for an investor is to organize information. This is broken down into 5 parts.

    1. Identify the news sources that forecast a country's economic forecast. Obviously we'll be using the US because of the

ability to access sound investment reports.

2. Identify long term profit potentials and understand which major markets are secure long term allowing an investor to make confident short term investments. Examples of this are, infrastructure, renewable energy and technology.
3. Identify sources that release sound reports on innovations, trends, business acquisitions and IPOs inside of a market.
4. Identify sound businesses inside of a proven market that have promising growth indicators.
5. Using technical analysis to capitalize on consistently strong investment opportunities.

Yes accurate reports exist inside of every aspect of investing listed above. The most valuable asset in the modern era is where a people place their attention. The more wealthy the individual is, then more that individual's attention is worth. The more valuable the information provided a wealthy individual, the more profitable its authority and reputation is. Investment publications and news sources always remember this and it is in their only interest to produce quick and easy access to profits for the world's smartest investors.

The Big Takeaway From This Section
All this information sounds broad, theoretical and a little bit complicated with incomplete and unspecific trading tactics.So what was the point of this Module?

The answer is simple:
As a modern investor, it's crucial to take

advantage of every asset available.

The biggest three assets to a modern investor are:
1. The ability to fine tune and optimize current money management to free up insane amounts over long term profits.
2. To understand the value of a currency and the importance of using every currency as wisely as possible. There is no substitute for great budgeting and is the beginning of sound investing.
3. To announce a very basic introduction of the important tools used in modern investing. By using time and focus optimally and understanding the value of attention, it's easier to use every resource available to your advantage.

This module is the first step in creating your

Profit Playbook. Remember to create a budget. Mint is phenomenal financial tracker but the choice is yours. Your action step is to find the best deal you can for every $ you invest. If you spend a lot of time and money on entertainment, find ways to cut costs and invent new ways to spend your time and entertain yourself.

Just remember by taking action now, you're building your Profit Playbook with a foundation to wealth while every step skipped in Beginner's Profit Playbook diminishes the structure of a wealth portfolio and will ultimately lead to financial collapse. By building and refining your budget, you're well on your way to a wonderful, well deserved reward for the money that's been earned through the weeks, months and years of hard work.

Up next is the breakdown of financial markets and the foundations to any consistently successful trading strategy.

Part 2:

The Journey to Becoming a Forex Pro

The Golden Ticket

Before we dive into the successful trading strategies, it's important to understand that there's a huge difference between professional traders from the rest of the world. This text was designed with the sole intention of taking a beginner or struggling trader and giving that trader the tools necessary to make consistent income then continue to use that income to accumulate wealth through economic booms and depressions. But as we set of on an adventure of a life time, invest $10,000s and spend 1000s of hours of hard work to build a fantastic career as a Forex trader, it might be a good idea to ask a quick question.

"What separates a professional trader from the other 99.99% of traders fighting for their lives to salvage an income through trading Forex?"

The Keys to the Kingdom of Professional Trading:

You probably have heard this before, but the secret to success, surprisingly has nothing to do with shiny and "exotic" trading strategies that rule the online trading world. There are hundreds of trading strategies that work incredibly well in Forex. Sadly though, a small number (.01%) of Forex students turn professional. Just this simple statistic alone makes it crystal clear that trading strategies are a tiny piece to the puzzle of becoming a professional trader.

Throughout this book, you'll be introduced to the world of professional trading that will give you the foundations to make consistent profit through trading the foreign exchange market. Trading for a living comes through building an empire one brick at a time and the very first and most important first building block to becoming a profitable professional is to ultimately understand how pros operate.

A professional trader can take the simplest trading strategy and accumulate a long-term fortune.Similarly, amateurs can lose an entire life savings using the best systems known to man.

As a new trader hops into the realm of Forex without formal training, it's comparable to a fan walking up to bat against Mariano Rivera with a World Series title on the line. The results would be nothing but havoc; but don't fret. Unlike the Major Leagues, anyone with an internet connection can quickly become a profitable pro right off the bat.

This is because the key to accumulating wealth in trading is understanding that every trading strategy and every trading system loses trades on a consistent basis.

When a losing streak inevitably hits a profitable system, professional traders simply roll through these trades un-phased and completely confident as they continue to make the same trade 100 times. After 100 trades, the trader cherishes his or her discipline and lives in the life of profits. Traders that ultimately fail, naturally feel like there is something wrong after they lose money after a week of scanning currencies and executing perfect trades. In turn, they begin to question their strategies and begin to execute trades at the wrong times and to pull out of successful trades to early transforming a profit to a loss. The key in professional trading is to analyze potential trades through a proven system, to execute the trade properly, and to have faith through the inevitable fluxes that rule the world of Forex.

Acquiring Nerves of Steel:

It's pretty easy to relate professional traders to superheroes. They have the discipline of champions and in times of adversity, they exhibit nerves of steel. Trading live can be hard when life savings and chances for financial independence are on the line; but when pros walk up to the trading station, the pressure of a better life doesn't exist. Professionals stay patient every day and never sway from their trading strategies. They use EXACT indicators inside of very specific conditions and never relinquish the trading strategies that fill accounts with long term profits.

It's easy for a trader to learn and understand a trading strategy but what separates winning traders from losing traders is the ability to follow every trading strategy, exactly. As a professional scans the forex market, he or she can encounter hundreds of trading conditions in a day without making a single trade. During the same day while using the same strategy, an amateur can pull 4 or 5 trades that are almost perfect in nature, but are not exactly buying triggers. And these "almost perfect trades" can end the dreams of an aspiring novice to transform into a professional trader.

This fact is simple. While there are thousands of successful trading strategies floating through the internet, there is only ONE road to becoming a Pro.

This is through the identification of an exact trading strategy and the

perfect execution of that strategy EXACTLY.

Every other hopeful path to the world of FOREX leads to a financial apocalypse.

The Only Wealth Manufacturer of Forex:

There's no feeling like the moment a trader goes live for the first time. As a first time a person clicks the buy button, years of sacrifice and hard work become meaningless. The money invested is wagered inside the vast and completely random $5,000,000,000,000 ocean of daily trade volume that brings the foreign exchange world to life. As this happens, a trader quickly learns that there's no replacement for the discipline required strictly follow a trading strategy in real-time. This exact situation leads us to the first trading strategy that's required in becoming a professional currency trader.

Strategy #1: Creating a personal Trading Periodical.

It'll likely be a hot minute before you go begin live trading inside of Forex and a lot of brilliance goes into the swift moment that a trader makes an order in Forex. In these conditions, only a trader with a solid foundation in trading fundamentals is destined to become profitable. Like any other type of professional gambler, a trader is very organized and brilliantly methodical when building wealth through Forex. Forex is a phenomenal wealth engine but there's always a catch high volume markets like the Foreign Exchange. Exceptional trading opportunities happen because of trading volume. But sadly, high trade volume creates high volatility and even the most intelligent humans get confused by combining money and volatility.

Humans are genetically designed with an unparalleled attention to detail, but our gifts come with a catch. Attention to detail becomes immediately present when we put a life-line at risk and there's an argument that large amounts of money is crucial life-line in modern culture. Without money, we have a high probability to die. This means that a new trader is wired to think in terms of immediate results as they begin a professional trading career.

Luckily, this happens to everyone because we're human and instead of fighting it, we're going to utilize this human nature to our advantage.

Creating a Trading Periodical:

Think of a trading periodical like your very own professional trading journal. You use your periodical to report the exact emotions and thoughts you first encountered and then used as information to form a decision. This journal will be used to identify your strengths and weaknesses in spotting healthy trading environments, identifying correct trading opportunities and using your exact trading strategies to correctly execute consistently profitable trades. As time flies by at your "trading station", you'll begin to understand that your periodical has easily become the most powerful tool you will ever own as a trader. But for now, we'll start the periodically simply. This will allow rapid profit generation for beginning and struggling traders.

A trading periodical analyzes 4 main sections inside of every trading session:

1. Scanning Forex
2. Identifying Trading Opportunities.
3. Executing Trading Opportunities.
4. Managing Live Trades

Every time you engage a chart, you must document use these 4 tools to interview and report to your periodical and it must be done under the appropriate section listed above.

Exact Time:

Currency Pair/ Time Frame:

Feeling(s): (don't explain mentally. Just say exact feeling and emotion)

Thought(s): mental decisions that lead to you engaging within a chart

....

You'll leave the 5th report blank until you go back and analyze your trading session report. The 5th report is: Jump back into your memory, identify your thoughts and gain control of your attention to perfectly execute the trade in your imagination.

Examples of engaging with your chart include:

-Every time you adjust your trading charts(ex: opening a new one or zooming into a single pair or out of a single or few currency pairs.)
-Every time you identify a trading opportunity.
-Every time you follow a trading opportunity.
-Every time you execute a trade.

-Every time you exit a trade.

-Constantly looking at a pair you have a live trade in is also important to document. Fidgets like zooming in to check on your trade's profits or feeling nervous about other trading opportunities while you have a live trade are important to identify.

Analyzing every Trading Session

After every day is done, reflect on your journal. You'll notice a lot of weird, uncontrollable emotions and it's important to understand them and reaffirm correct thoughts, emotions and actions.

For example: Let's say you had the urge to watch a profitable trade. As this trade become more and more profitable you might have felt the urge to pull your trade for a win or save a winning trade when your profits start to cut back.

This is totally natural. Just remember that you have a trading strategy that's in place to eliminate all the confusion that comes with managing a trade.

Every report in your periodical has one use. To identify when you followed trading strategies properly and when you let your emotions and thoughts get the best of you. You can then use this information to go back into those memories and imagine doing the proper thing and to mentally create the exact outcomes that would have occurred during a perfectly executed trade.

For example:

If you jumped into a trade too early, go back to your report of the trade and relive the trade as if the thought or emotion just sparked. Remember your system, regain control of your attention and execute the trade perfectly as the trade develops. After you finish visualizing say to yourself "The only way to become a professional trader is by exactly following my trading strategy. The feelings/thoughts of (say thoughts or feelings report) I encountered during this trade are natural reactions in trading. When I encounter these thoughts emotions in the future, I'll identify them and remember to execute the trade perfectly like I just did in my memory."

The more you do this, the more you not only gain control of your emotions. Over time, you'll ingrain successful trading habits and you'll master the execution of your trading set ups into your memory and subconscious. However, this can only occur through repetition. This strategy results in securing your future success more and more with every documentation inside of your periodical.

Part 3:
The Profitable Power of Risk Management

Risk Management

Even if a trader successfully uses and applies a trading periodical, he or she can still go broke without using the proper strategies that are required as a professional. To eliminate this cost of destruction inside of your aspirations, Risk Management becomes a fundamental tool towards becoming a professional Forex trader. Odds, statistics and probabilities can create some extreme volatility throughout the course of a decade. Even a trading strategy that wins 90% of the time can "impossibly" and "uncontrollably" lose 50 times in a row throughout an extremely rough time period. Sound absurd? It's important to understand this can happen to traders that makes only 10,000 trades over a decade. And as crazy as it sounds, 50 losses would only account for 5% of the losses during series of 10,000 trades. If you make 5 trades a day for 5 years straight, that puts you at 9,125 trade executions. The money that's available inside of the foreign exchange market sounds exciting, but the market is lit with an unforgiving lash of volatility. Volatility is dangerous in Forex and has ended countless trading careers. It's important that you never take your optimism for granted. It's possible to become a pro, but you have to use sound risk management practices to protect yourself from going broke. Therefor, it's crucial for you to protect yourself during the most epic volatility.

As a new or struggling trader, there are two proven ways to battle the gods of volatility. It's important to take advantage of both for protection. The first strategy for investing money safely is by designing or using proven, consistent, safe systems and to specifically track every trade to maximize your probabilities of winning. The second way to battle volatility comes from saving your financial freedom is through risk management. A losing spell strikes every pro throughout his or her career and it's obviously crucial to make sure you're ready for it. Over time, a simplistic but true pro stays safe while extremely skilled amateurs go bankrupt.

There are two options to become profitable out the gate as a new trader.

1. You can back test proven strategies with software so the trader has faith in the exact system out the gates. No one knows when a system will win or lose which means there is no substitution for confidence. Knowing a system is proven, allows any trader to hit the ground running and allows to a trader to confidently invest up to .5-1% of your total investing account as a beginner. As you build your account balance, it's best to scale back to .25%-.5% to protect both your income and your career. Document exact entry points, the exact reason each trade was entered and the exact system used to manage and ultimately exit the trade. Review trades both daily & weekly to ensure that you're properly executing your trades.

2. This is a favorite option for new traders because it allows live trading immediately with little risk. Pick a proven system inside this course then immediately start trading .1-.2% of the trader's account fund. Document exact entry points, the exact reason each trade was entered and the exact system used to manage and ultimately exit the trade. Review trades daily & weekly to ensure you're properly executing your trades.

As a trader gains confidence inside of a system, trades can be executed at 1-2% of the trader's funds inside his or her account portfolio. However, it's important to understand that professional rarely trades over 1% of their account funds and NEVER exceeds 2% in a single trade. This type of risk management keeps the best traders in the world afloat. No one can win every time but only pros make it through loosing weeks with confidence and they never waiver from their risk management. EVER. NEVER EVER.

PROS BUILD WEALTH LONG-TERM.

PROFESSIONALS NEVER TRADE MORE THAN 2% OF THE FUNDS IN YOUR ACCOUNT.

EXECUTING A TRADE THAT INVESTS MORE THAN 2% OF ACCOUNT FUNDS KILLS FINANCIAL LIFE-LINES.

INSTEAD:
CREATE RAPID PROFITS BY INCREASING MONTHLY ROI THROUGH ADDITIONS OF HIGH PROBABILITY TRADING STRATEGIES THAT OCCUR FREQUENTLY AND CONTINUE TO UTILIZE LOW RISK/HIGH REWARD OPPORTUNITIES.

MASTER EVERY STRATEGY BEFORE TRADING IT LIVE.
&
ALWAYS REFERENCE THE EXACT TRADING RULES AND PICTURES WHEN EXECUTING A TRADING STRATEGY.
IF YOU'RE UNSURE ABOUT A TRADE, NEVER BUY. SOMETHING IS

PROBALY WRONG WITH YOUR SET-UP

....

ANALYZE EVERY TRADE AFTER EVERY SESSION USING A TRADING PERIODICAL & ALWAYS STAY SAFE.

Part 4: The Basics of Reading a Forex Chart

Reading a Forex Chart

Looking at a Forex chart for the first time can be incredibly intimidating but all will be good after this brief introduction. There are an insane number of different types of bars and trading platforms that are loaded with hundreds of indicators that can overwhelm even the most brilliant men and women in the world. The good news is that they are actually really easy to understand and navigate. So it's alright to take a deep breath and let out a nice sigh of relief. After you understand the basics, the infinite stats inside the forex climate will quickly turn into a wonderful map to creating sustainable wealth.

The Most Important Currency Pairs:

You already know that Forex is a place where people exchange one currency for another but how do you understand and navigate through the Forex market from your computer? Well we start by understanding pairs or the chart of two currencies weighed against each other.

There a four major pairs in forex:
EUR/USD (euro/dollar) – "euro"
USD/JPY (U.S. dollar/Japanese yen) – "gopher"
GBP/USD (British pound/dollar) - "cable"
USD/CHF (U.S. dollar/Swiss franc) –

"swissie"

And there are three smaller players:

AUD/USD (Australian dollar/U.S. dollar) – "aussie"

USD/CAD (U.S. dollar/Canadian dollar) – "loonie"

NZD/USD (New Zealand dollar/U.S. dollar) – "kiwi

Note the currency on the left is the primary currency and the currency on the right is the currency weighing against the primary currency on the left side.

-It's alright to use any currency pairs but these top 7 are the most stable and therefor create higher probabilities for winning trades.

QUICKLY NAVIGATING A FOREX CHART

It's always important to understand what you're looking at when you see a chart and honestly, the first time you glimpse at a naked Forex Chart, what you'll see is pretty simplistic so let's break it down and then move on to the next module.

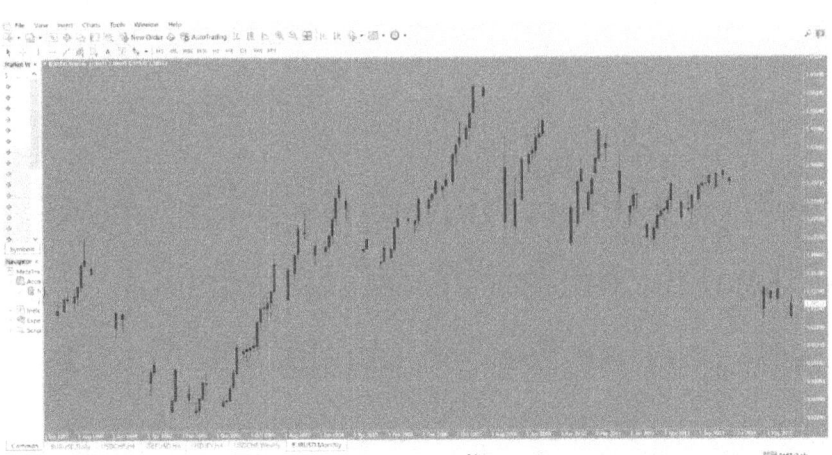

So you know what you're looking at, trading platforms always display name of the pair in the top left corner of the chart (EUR/USD). As you're looking at a currency pair, you'll also find another key feature so you can navigate through a currency pair like a pro.

This feature is the time table..

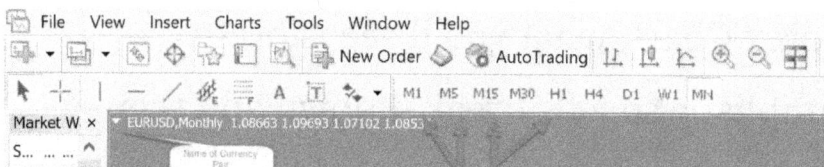

The blue arrows in the picture above point to the time tables for the currency pair you look at.

The time frames in the picture above are M1-MN and the time-table options you have access to are typically 1 minute, 5 minute, 15 minute, 30 minute, 1 hour, 4 hour, 1 day, 1 week and 1 year intervals.

When you select or click a time frame, each candlestick represents the time you selected. The previous chart was selected monthly so every candlestick would represent a month. Simple enough.

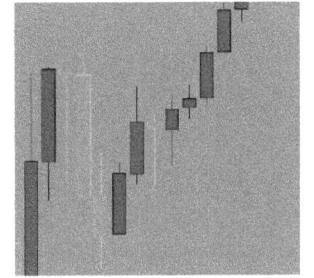

But what is a candlestick?

How to Read a Candlestick: Candlesticks are a very simple but powerful way to display price and is recommended as the only tool to display price.

Each candlestick in a chart represent a time frame.

Every candlestick uses 4 main price points.

1. The highest price that occurred inside of the candlestick

2. The lowest price that occurred inside the candlestick

3. The price the candlestick opened with.

4. The price the candlestick closed with.

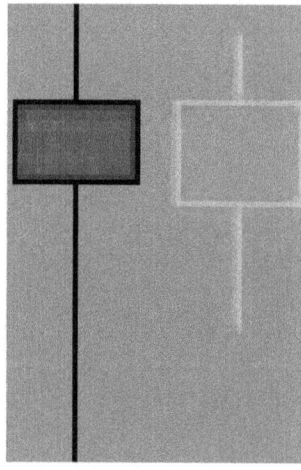

The spikes or wicks in a candle represent the highest and lowest price traded during the candlestick's time frame.

The boxes simply represent the opening and

closing prices during the time period of the candlestick.

In this example, if a candlestick is green, the candle moved upwards. If a candle is red, the candle closed at a price lower than the candle's opening price.

Forex Climates:

After seeing and understanding the two previous examples, you've learned how to read candlesticks over a series of time. Congratulations, because this is the foundation of every trading strategy inside almost every profitable trading system. Now that we understand how to read a Forex chart, it's time to understand that there are two major types of climates Foreign Exchange lives in. That way we know how each climate works as we dive into our trading strategies throughout the course.

The first type of climate currency pairs live in is called a Trend:

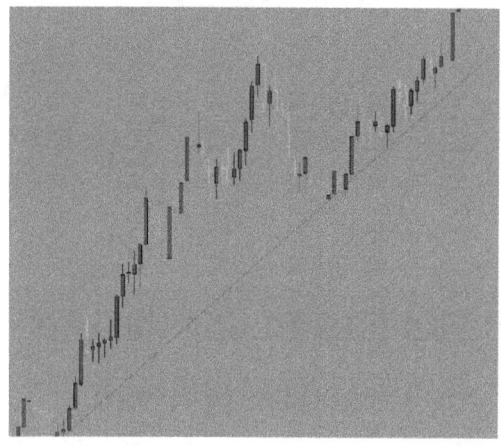

A trend happens when one currency consistently rises or falls against another throughout a period of time.

Trends tend to hold measurable momentum

throughout a time period creating a safe trading environment for all traders.

This makes the trending climate a trader's best friend. Trends are perfect for executing high probability trades with low risks and high rewards.

Price Action and Moving Averages are the best trading tools inside of a climate that's trending.

The second type of climate is called a Range:

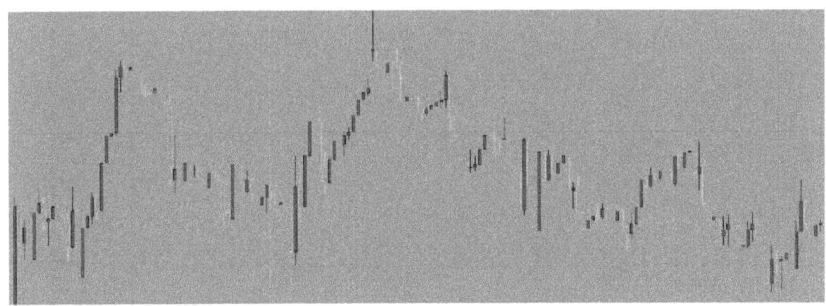

A Range climate happens when a currency

pair stays within a high price point and a low price point for an extended period of time. In the example above, you can see the price consistently try to break out into a trending climate but the market clearly settles back into a clearly defined range of prices over a long period of time.

The main type of trading indicators used inside of a range climate are Bollinger Bands and Average Directional Index (ADX)

Tracking Market Movement:

The last aspect of this section is to realize that there is only one job as an individual trader.

And the job is simple:

Use high volume, high momentum, and breakout patterns to invest into micro portions of the massive market.

Currency is a tricky game if you try to understand exactly what's happening. So instead, we'll just keep things simple to make our profits.

It's suggested that the most successful systems are not built from predicting initial movements of momentum. However, beginner traders can consistently utilize the advantages inside of market movement, market momentum, and market volume to create fantastic highly profitable trading opportunities. But why do these basic and simple strategies work in the first place?

The answer is actually very simple

The job of an individual trader is to take advantage of Institutional traders trading volumes. This helps identify momentum and market direction.

A primary example occurs through 30 and 50 SMA (Simple Moving Averages)

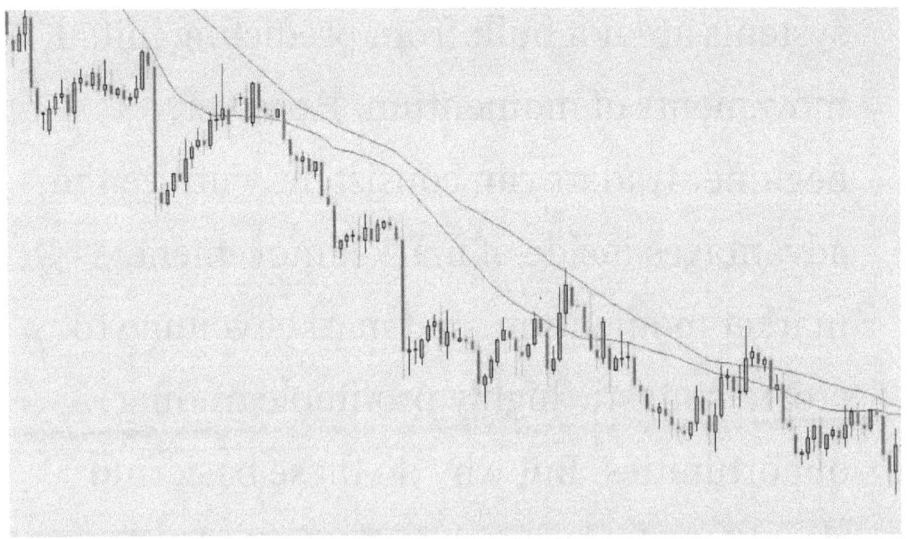

Throughout this trend, 30/50 SMA lines were used as major support levels for institutional traders to invest their money which leaves the gate wide open for individual traders to execute higher probability trades.

Dozens of successful trades can be made inside of these trends which helps individual traders capitalize on short-term security through the major players that are in charge of moving the long-term market.

In the next part, we'll begin to understand indicators so we can find healthy trading climates and identify the types of trades that have high chances of winning.

But before you go live, make sure you make

your Trading Periodical a part of your trading practice. It alone will define your luck and profits throughout your trading career.

Part 5:
The Power Of Framing

What in the world is framing?

As a beginner at currency trading, it's important to execute a lower amount of trades that have a higher probability of winning. This will steeply decrease the learning curve that comes with serious trading and eases the nerves that come when embarking on your journey to become financially independent.

And while framing is powerful, it's important to understand that no trade works 100% of the time. As you begin trading you may feel tempted to invest a lot more than 2% on a trade that's practically guaranteed to win but the truth is that no system, ever, is 100% successful.

Volatility is a brutal kingdom and the job of a beginner is to eliminate as much of it as possible. In order to do this, we're going to take up the science of framing.

Most experts call framing Multiple time frame analysis. It's the strategy that is consistently used by pros to check the odds that the signals they see on one time frame is working with the momentum of a long term trend. Framing is the first introduction into the power of momentum and can be responsible for the destruction of a good trade.

A perfect example comes as your cruising through a 5 minute chart. You start to see a trade forming and your trading system is giving you a nice go ahead to execute the trade you've been looking for a couple of hours. You praise your patience and perfectly execute the trade. But to your dismay, the trade quickly slaps against you and you encounter another loss. You're staying patient, executing the trades properly but for some reason, you are encountering far more than your system should be allowing.

What's happening?

Well, that lovely 5min chart that said the currency pair was a go, is likely stuck inside of a far bigger momentum. As you zoom out of your 5 minute chart, you'll begin to realize that you were trading against a trend that has been booming for a couple of weeks. In turn, the trade that you though was sound was actually a trade with high volatility. What you saw as a strong upwards trend was actually a bounce back on a long term down trend against the pair. If you're not careful, these conflicting momentum charts can bring a royal pain into your trading aspirations.

As a whole, professional traders truly do prefer to trade on different time frames and the fact of the matter is that no one time frame is perfect. Every chart has it's perks and drawbacks and every trader enjoys trading on different scales. However, one thing that most pro traders confirm as important is the overall market momentum over larger chart times.

So how do we take advantage of these longer time frames(4H and 1D) and use them in the shorter time frames(the 5M,15M and 1H)?

In a world where you have a million indicators ready to rock, it's best to simplify our strategy so that we can consistently make winning trades. The truth is that by trading against the long term market, you're taking your cute little fluffy friend and placing it into a bet against a monster. By using longer termed charts you'll be aligning the gods of Forex to work in your favor. And there's no better feeling than putting your hard earned money into a healthy market. If you're not careful with framing, you'll consistently find your "good looking" trades stall out because it's working against a force that's 100x more powerful. Using multiple time frames will likely pull you out of more loosing trades than any other strategy that's available to traders(barring your trading journal).

But before we get started, it's important to remember that no framing strategy works 100% of the time and that you should let the your currency pairs guide you through what time frame you should spend your trading session inside of.

How should you select good trading opportunities using time frames?

In the incredibly complicated world of foreign exchange, it's best to approach your trading simplistically.

When you start your session, you should look at the 7 major currency pairs from the 1 week chart and begin documenting where you see up trends, downtrends and ranges. Next switch over to the 1 day and document your analysis and then follow through documenting in the 4 hour, 1 hour, 30 minute 15 minute, 5 minute and 1 minute charts.

This is considered as a perfect way to start off your day. Without the understanding of where you have momentum inside the currency market, you'll never be able to profitably pull your trading system to make it profitable over a long term basis.

After you document every chart, find where the currency charts have similar traits inside of 3 time frames.

Examples include:

-An up trend across of the 1 week, 1 day, and 4 hour charts inside of the same currency.
-A range across of the 1 day, 4 hour and 1 hour charts inside of the same currency.
-A downtrend across of the 1 hour, 30 minute

and 15 minute charts inside of the same currency.

Highlight all of the "same momentum" opportunities and begin your day inside of the smallest relating chart. It's also common to find charts that show the same traits across more than 3 time tables. If you happen to be inside of one of these opportunities, good for you! Begin your trading on the shortest time table and begin applying your trading strategies. Throughout a day, you may find multiple trades across multiple time tables for the same currency. You can capitalize on each individual trade and treat them as individual trade executions.

Characteristics of Time Frames:

Long Term Trades:

Large time frames typically include the 4 hour, daily and weekly time tables to execute trades. These trades provide high ROI opportunities but they do tend to take a while to develop. Common characteristics of the amount of time it takes to exit trades that occur on this level occur after weeks, months and even years depending on the momentum and exit strategy.

While these trades can pull in a ridiculous return, trading at this level requires an incredible amount of patience and discipline while executing this style of trade. You'll find that there are very few opportunities at this level(probably no more than 3 or 4 a year) and when you find a chance to pull the trigger, it could take weeks to execute the trade. After execution, you'll consistently find yourself in the midst of multiple month long loosing streaks and can suck up a huge amount of money. Long term traders typically have a tendency to have bigger pockets so they can combat the long term swings that can occur throughout year long trades.

Swing Trades:

Swing trading is considered as a middle ground between long term and intraday trading styles. Most swing traders prefer to execute trades at the hourly level and tend to hold on to the trades anywhere from a couple hours up to a week. Swing trading is considered as a sweet spot among most pros. This style of trading presents more consistent trade opportunities and will allow you to produce positive returns on a month to month basis. However, you'll notice that the spread will eat up some of the capital and overnight trading activity can wreck havoc on your trades if you're not careful.

Intraday Trades:

The intraday time table tends to be traded along the 15 minute to 1 minute charts. These trades typically take no more than a few hours to execute and almost always get executed before the trading session is finished. Due to the shorter time frames, you'll find yourself with a gold mind of opportunities to trade in. However, it's important to note that intraday trading is more volatile than swing trading. Due to this fact, you'll find lower percentage of wins. However, this can be balanced out through less long term volatility. Due to the number of trades produced at the intraday level, you'll fin that there's far less of a risk for netting a loosing month. However, you must be prepared to trade at this level. Trading can get crazy while operating on this level so you must stay disciplined and sharp throughout the trading day to become successful with this style of trading. Also, the margins on these trades are incredibly high in comparative to swing trading. Sometimes it'll feel like you're netting a lot of wins but you'll find yourself shorthanded due to the spreads.

As you begin to wonder what your preference on your sweet spot to execute trades, remind yourself that every trading style has its benefits and drawbacks. If you're trading long term, remember that you'll find yourself with ridiculous exit losses. In turn, intraday feels like a lot of work for a little bit of change but you'll find that your exit strategies are incredibly pocket friendly compared to long term.

However, no matter what time frame you choose, it should fit your personality. If you like to analyze a trade and make absolutely sure you'd like to enter trades, you can execute long term trades as well as longer swing trades to make sure you feel confident in your trade execution. However, if you can't stand to wait for weeks at a time to execute and exit a trade, short term swing trading and intraday trading will likely be for you. Just make sure you find your own groove before you go live. Your framing will ultimately determine what styles of trading and analysis you'll use over the long haul so be mindful for what matches your strength and what could kill your dreams to go pro. In order to make sure you match a style of trading, it's suggested by most institutions to run a 90 day DEMO before you go live. This will ensure that you're comfortable with your trading style, your trading system and your trading execution before you put your prized money on the line. When you settle in, you'll find that trading is a blast rather than a stressful and unstable financial roller coaster.

Part 6:
The Basics Of Price Action

The basics of price action are incredibly powerful fundamentals that almost all traders live by.

And while there are a million different styles to price action, they all have similar basics.

These include:

The State of the Market, which include up trends, down trends and ranges.

Support and Resistance Levels.

The state of the market is very easy to identify.

The market is in an up trend when the value of a currency pair is consistently rising.

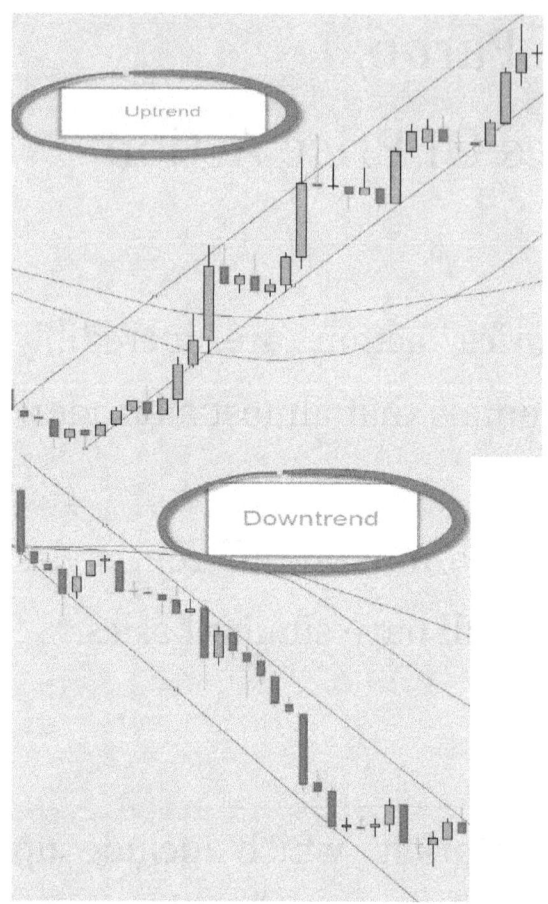

The market is in a down trend when the value of a currency pair is consistently falling.

The market is in a range when the price of a currency is stuck between a low point and a high point.

Support and resistance is very basic. The example below demonstrates the concept: Resistance is an "imaginary" price point a currency has trouble breaking through.

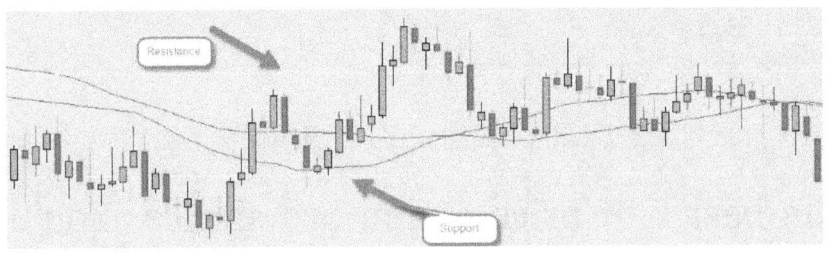

Support is an "imaginary" price point that a currency tends to bounce off of.

Support and resistance levels can occur on every level and they can be found in ranges, up trends, and down trends.

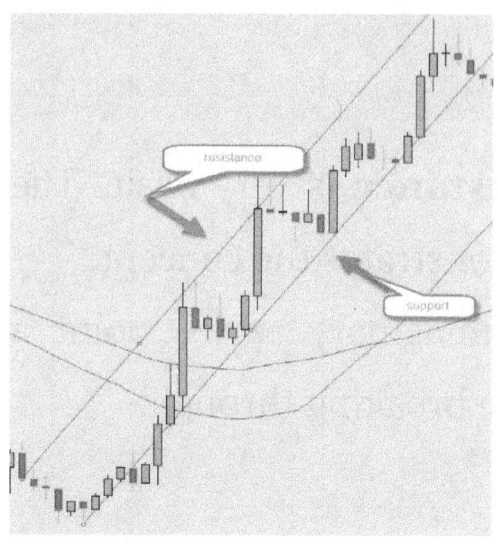

The basics of price action are simple. You'll find the market in only 3 states. An uptrend, a down trend or a range. While the market is inside of one of three states, it will be running off a level of support or resistance.

In price action, it's important to remember that framing plays a large role. The more often you see support in resistance in longer charts, the more important the support and resistance levels are.

~When a price breaks above or below the support or resistance level, it tends to move far beyond it's former resistance. This is considered as a "breakout."

~When a price bounces off a support or resistance level, it naturally moves in the opposite direction. This is considered a "bounce-back".

Therefor, most trades occur during breakouts and bounce-backs. However, take special care before jumping into these trades. Some potential break outs develop into bounce-backs and some bounce-backs develop into breakouts. These mixed signals happen quite often so in order to protect ourselves, we must have some way to identify when breakouts and bounce-backs are most likely to occur. This is done through using entry strategies.

Part 7:
How To Enter Profitable Trades

While there are a million ways to capitalize off of breakouts and bounce-backs, the main strategy for making money is incredibly simple when it comes to professional trading. A professional uses exact indicators to find high quality trades during major price fluctuations. High quality trades are considered as high probability trades with low risks and high rewards.

Sounds simple right?

That's because it is. All too often, beginner and struggling traders try to over complicate the foreign exchange market because they can't believe how simplistic the game of trading is when it's broken down to its core.

Sure, there are some advanced strategies that pull far more success than basic strategies. However, it's practically impossible for advanced strategies to ignore the basic principles that make up successful trading practices.

Making Trades Using High Probability Patterns

This section is simply an introduction to entry strategies. These trading strategies use basic fundamental patterns that heavily indicate the odds of a breakout or a bounce back. By coming to grips and practicing these simple practices you'll begin to understand the simple nature that is required on your journey to becoming a professional trader. This strategy was designed for a single purpose. To eliminate the needs for using crazy indicators and advanced technical analysis through executing simplistic but high probability trades. While these strategies are simple, they are effective. This creates the perfect foundation for building your career as a professional trader. It builds initial discipline and allows you to settle into your trading sessions with confidence.

Pros believe that trading isn't about utilizing ultra advanced indicators and groundbreaking strategies. It's about finding simple, reproductive methods that match your personality and budget.

Here are a few basic patterns that will bring you long term stability while you dip your toes into the world of Forex.

Remember to always start your session by documenting the state of the market across every time table. This will allow you to develop a nice overall feel for where currency pairs are due for bigger breakouts and bounce-backs. When you come into your trading session prepared, you'll identify false breakouts because you understand the larger picture of every currency pair you're trading for.

As you're cruising through the market place, look for specific trading patterns presented below:

1. Symmetrical Triangle Breakouts

These trades offer an incredibly low risk while leaving room for high opportunities for breakouts. This continuation pattern is can be found in markets that are already inside of a trending market state. During an up trend, a triangle is created through decreasing prices along the resistance level and increasing prices along the support levels. The support and resistance then converge into a single point indicating the market is about ready to encounter a "big bang" in momentum. These triangles can also form during a down trend.

***Triangles can also be found in ascending or descending fashions. This occurs when a trend can't breakout from a level of resistance. However, the support of the trend continues to climb to new levels by bouncing of the support levels. Ultimately, the support and resistance levels converge into a single point. Once again, this sparks a high likely hood of a "big bang" inside of the currency.

For more information on triangle trading patterns, click here! Forex.com is a pretty cool place to gain some free trading knowledge

2.   Flag Breakouts.

Flag patterns are considered as a more powerful trade than triangles. When a currency pair enters an up trend, every pro trader is hopeful that it's the beginning of a "flag pole" as the momentum dies down. Flag patterns happen when a trend breaks out into a very specific range. Believe it or not, the flag is more powerful if it encounters a bounce-back against the initial trend. If you happen to spot this type of pattern, keep your eyes peeled for a breakout back into the trend's original direction.

For more information on flag breakouts, click [here](). Daily FX is a monster when it comes to education. Feel free to dive into their library of knowledge!

3. Pennant Breakout.

Pennant Breakouts are often considered by pros as the most powerful trading pattern in existence. It is a combination of the flag and the symmetrical triangle but with a little twist. Pennants break out within two bounces off of the currency pair's resistance and two bounces off of its support.

For more information on Pennant Breakouts, click [here.](#) Babypips is a wonderful place to learn more about Forex trading but beware of complicating things too quickly.

WHEN TO ENTER YOUR TRADES:

Now that you understand a couple of high risk and low reward patterns, it's time to learn when to pull the trigger.

There are 3 main strategies you can use when trying to trade a breakout pattern.

1. You can wait for the breakout to close above the latest point of resistance.

2. You can wait for the breakout to close past point of resistance that occurred during the breakout pattern. But in a lower time table.

3. You can wait for the breakout to CLOSE past the latest point of resistance.

Every style of trading has their benefits and drawbacks:

The first strategy is the most aggressive which means that it is less likely to produce a winning trade. However, using this style of play will allow you to hop in on the "bang" as early as possible with relatively little risk.

The second strategy is a little more conservative by nature but it's still a little risky without producing much of a benefit. This strategy can be used if a lower time table has closed out above the triangle. While this entry is still a little risky, it allows you to jump in with a little more confidence and still allows you to jump on the bandwagon to capitalize on the prized breakout.

The third strategy is considered as insanely stable. If the breakout closes above the latest point of resistance in a single bar, you have an incredibly high probability of winning the trade. Using this strategy in a pennant breakout is considered as the best high yield, high probability pattern trade possible.

Minimizing the risk of your trade by using a stop.

The foreign exchange market can absolutely obliterate your trading budget inside of a single "promising" trade. The moves can be unpredictable. In order to minimize the amount of money you can loose, all you need to do is set a price in which your trade automatically sells in a loss. This price point is commonly referred to by traders as a stop. Setting a perfect stop for your trade is best way for you to optimize your chances of successfully winning every trade while minimizing the amount of money you can loose when the market turns against you. The truth is that most trading systems don't win 80% of the time, but balancing out your risk and rewards will ultimately trigger a successful trader. If your risk to reward ratio is 4/1 but your winning rate is a casual 50%, statistics state that you'll, on average, double your money across every 4 trades. If you trade 1% of your available money, you'll double your trading account, on average, every 100 trades.

This is why the patterns above present such a powerful opportunity for you as you begin your journey into successful investing. Each of the patterns listed in this section generate trading opportunities that are very low in risk, very high in reward and very likely to develop into a winning trade.

But where do you actually place your stops?

Just like the entry, there are three fundamental exit strategies.
1. The first is the most conservative. It generates the lowest risk but a side effect is an increased number of losses. It places the stop slightly below the last point of support.
2. The second strategy places a stop slightly below the beginning of the pattern that's breaking out. The increase in odds of winning are directly related to a higher risk. However, this is considered as the

most optimal strategy by most pros.

3. The third strategy is by far the most risky. The stop is placed slightly below the last level of support that occurred before the trend ended. This protects traders in case of a false bounce-back. However, the losses are huge comparative to the first and second strategies. The increased risk doesn't substitute enough to balance out the gain in your odds of winning your trade.

Trailing Stops:

After you've successfully capitalized on a breakout, it's time to celebrate your patience by consistently moving your stop loss into profits.

After your currency breaks out in a positive fashion, there are a couple of ways you can move your stop. Like all strategies, every approach has its perks and drawbacks.

1. You can use the average true range index. This exit strategy is pretty well rounded. It allows the trader to exit the trade once the momentum dies. However, this exit strategy could miss out on a good portion of the trend; but unlike the second exit strategy, average true range can get you out of a trade at the top of a trend.

2. You can use a stop that's slightly placed below the latest bounce-back inside of your trend. This is by far the most aggressive strategy for trailing stops. This stop produces the highest chances to ride out extremely long trends. This exit strategy allows a trader to ride almost every uptrend until the last leg(the top of the trend), while requiring the trader to always loose the entire last leg of every single trend.

3. You can raise your stop simultaneously with your gains. You can automate this style of stopping so that you can set and forget your trade. However, this exit strategy can cause traders to exit before the trend is finished.

Part 9:

You're Ready for Your First Trade

Are you excited?

This book presented the key tools to becoming a professional trader inside of the foreign exchange market. And while you may feel you've been denied a thorough approach in trading strategies, the simple strategies that have been presented are more than suitable to get you started inside your journey to becoming a pro.

Always remember to use your trading periodical like you do your grooming habits. It will allow you to thrive while you become a professional and will give you a competitive edge as your trading triggers your survival mechanisms that naturally occur when you put a financial life line at risk. Never risk higher than 2% of your total trading bank and always remember to stick to the basics of finding successful trades.

As you begin to fine tune and advance your trading strategies, ensure you stay true to the fundamentals. There are millions of trading strategies out there and the strategies that ignore the basics should be considered as high risk trading strategies. Advanced market algorithms should only be used as a further indicator for basic price action principles that ultimately rule Forex.

FOR MORE INFORMATION ON TRADING PATTERNS, CHECK OUT THESE FREE SCHOOLS TO GUIDE YOU TO SUCCESS:

https://www.dailyfx.com/forex-education

https://www.forex.com/en-us/education/

http://www.babypips.com/school

These sites use the proper foundations to teach their trading strategies. Therefore, they are trusted to produce winning traders on a consistent basis. While you're encouraged to find a mentor, everything you need to become a pro has been presented in this book and in the free resources above.

www.ingramcontent.com/pod-product-compliance
Lightning Source LLC
Chambersburg PA
CBHW061148180526
45170CB00002B/675